PERDITION

PERDITION

Part One of
The Profane Comedy

by D. Selby Fing

Washington, DC

Copyright © 2020 D. Selby Fing

Art copyright (interior and cover) © 2020 Seth Goodkind

New Academia Publishing 2020

All rights reserved. No part of this book may be reproduced or transmitted in any form or by any means, electronic or mechanical, including photocopying, recording, or by any information storage and retrieval system.

Printed in the United States of America

Library of Congress Control Number: 2020912439
ISBN 978-1-7348659-4-3 (alk. paper)

   An imprint of New Academia Publishing

   New Academia Publishing
4401-A Connecticut Avenue NW #236, Washington DC 20008
info@newacademia.com - www.newacademia.com

Inspired by

Robert Zimmerman
Charles Thompson
Aaron Freeman and
Mickey Melchiondo

For Kim Sook

2 - A path appears to be a web.

One's journey goes a certain distance
When a path appears to be a web.　　　　　　　　(2)
To be content in such an instance

Would seem like halting the tidal ebb.
There are so few means to one's assistance.
The first step is the one we most dread;

No single strand can support one's ambition,
No direction appeals to curiosity,
No reason can surmount the fearful vision

That pride has positioned into apostasy.
All around the spiders of excision
Threaten to put cease to our velocity,

Yet the duty to vocation reckons
To propel us forward, despite our wishes.
One has no choice but to be beckoned,

And to taste the bitter as delicious.
Still I sat for an ocean of contemplative seconds
And I meditated upon the oily, viscous

Feeling of this muck of indecision.
I tried to hold it gently in my hands,
The fabric of my life so tawdry thin,

I had no power to resume a graceful stance
Against the buffeting winds of adversion,
To speculate and gamble against chance,

When one did come before me I well knew,
Furrowed mottled sorrow on his brow,
The passion of my apathy flew

Yet he was some ghost before me now.
His eyes were as black as the sun is blue.
I kept no doubt abiding anyhow;

Beside my empty contemplation, he held
Out the calloused softness of his palm.
Not smiling but seething a strength I felt,

Exuding both a vulgar and divine calm,
The man could not be pelted with insult,
And so his apparition caused no alarm.

I: "Sir, you are both humble and exalted.
Please tell me how it is you've come before me."
He shook his head as if I could not be faulted,

Mistaking him for someone with greater glory.
He: "Son, please do let your wonder be halted.
For I am not a martyr in my story."

"But sir, you are emblazoned on my money!"
And I reached inside my purse to verify.
I showed the bill and coinage, he said, "Funny,   (45)

45 - I showed the bill and coinage, he said, "Funny."

I always find the need to clarify
That even as I do not pray on Sunday,
To no religion of myself can I testify."

I: "And yet you stand as representative
Of ideals which good citizens may pursue.
I know you need to be modestly tentative,

But coyness on your part wouldn't be true."
I was trying his patience and being inelegant.
"I offered my hand, where I could have withdrew."

Pleading, "Sorry," I said, "I just can't believe it.
May I ask you a few simple questions?"
"I am Lincoln, young man, can you not conceive it?"

I was afraid to respond with further investigations.
So I put my hand out to leave there:
"Do you know a way out of this vivisection?"

"There is no way out," but he grinned and he snickered,
As if he was aware of what was to come.
I looked as his unblue-unblack eyes flickered.

He: "But you must better know what has gone.
For in this desperate state you have been snookered.
You very simply don't know what's been done."

I wavered slightly at his abrupt suggestion.
I learned despite my teachers, all I knew of truth.
I bought no lies, have always been an exception,

Who dares to tell me what I must pursue?
Incredibly, it was Abraham Lincoln.
He noted the labyrinth of my thought, "Forsooth,

Who taught you to always so depend upon yourself?
Be patient, I will show you what human can mean.
By this manner you may experience yourself;

Your part in the whole." He convinced and we proceeded   (76)
Along the thinnest strand of the web, which felt
As if it were as wide as the open seas.

76 - ...your part in the whole.

And which reverberated with every step.
In motion, but supporting our motion as well.
I might have been the length of an insect

Quivering on the kissing breezes swell,
Or the very wind itself, the path was set
Before us like the telling tolling of a bell.

I followed, unbelieving of the import
But hungry for a good story to tell.
I thought to summon up some witty retort

But, by a strange misstep, my guide fell.
I took his wrist and helped raise my consort.
Quoth my uncle: "Good thing it wasn't a well."

I looked at him, but then we reached the gateway,
The sign on the stile, 'Here is morality.'   (92)
The path appeared to continue straightaway,

But that is not what it was in reality
For the structure of our steps faded away
And we both dropped down immediately

To the first level of the passages
Through the red hallowed annals of history –
In the life that we lived as the hostages

92 - Here is morality.

Of the rationally disciplined mystery
Of Ben Franklin's most loving adages.
And I was scared at what I was about to see.

He: "Do not stray from my side, this blankness
Is only the will of the other.
I tell you in all understated frankness,

As if you were to become my brother,
You must let go of your lankness
And remember that you have no mother,

Other than the one who brings us together."
I: "But what are we about to see here?"
"A graveyard of promises strewn with heather.

What has been left behind is held most dear,
And as easily retained as ether
While the vacuum of that space is filled with fear.

Do not be afraid of the vacuum, young man."
But for the scarlet liquidity and heat, the vacuum
Was all, I could feel it in my cast iron frying pan.

I was penetrated with sweat and my rectum
Loosened in anticipation of Satan's imminence.
My guide seemed in need of no diction

To read the flash of fear's imagination
Upon my confused visage. He shook his head.
Said: "I trust you not to panic in action.

Nothing that you can see will make you bleed.
Do not allow yourself to be shaken in passion
Here at the beginning of a journey to the dead."

I barely said, "The dead?!" when a spuming fountain   (127)
Of regurgitation appeared before us
In the form of a gelified, jowled man

127 - ...a spuming fountain of regurgitation...

Whose bile reeked of the acid odor of
Self-deception, of the lie writ large on foul land.
He barely could speak for his esophagus

Was gushing an endless flow of noxious chunks.
My guide stood and waited with patient command.
The third: "I am the gatekeeper." The phlegm and reflux

Kept him from speaking, but he waved his hand –
Muttering "Mommy, Mommy," as piles soon built up –
As if to tell us to wait for him; it was hard to stand.

He stopped for a moment and turned to us with a grin
"Ronald Reagan, Mister Lincoln, nice to meet you."
My uncle did not hold out his hand, but kept his chin

Held to his chest and his brow remained dubious.
As the Old Biffer began to chork again,
I needed to question my guide, whose fury was

Well-contained in the cross-pins of his felt vest.
"I beg you to hold your questions just now, my son.
Here is a man who is nearly beside himself."

He waited silent 'til that greasy pate was done
Sickening up his lungs. I smelled his bilious belch.
I had to stand up straight after that one,

And speak up to say, "Why are you here?"
But my uncle chastised me, "Mr. President,"
By ignoring me and leaving me to fear,

In the manner of the child most innocent,
A further venting of his frustration later.
His scowl and reproach were without precedent,

In the mild justice which righteousness bestows
When tempered by the ideals of free institutions
In the glance of a man who you know who knows,

Having named the ideal in crystal distillation.
"Is there any sort of formality for us to go?"
Reagan's breath scorched our eyebrows and even

Caused my guide to turn his head and catch his wind.
"All are free to pass through here, none are in need
To offer justification," he said, "for their sin."

My teacher: "So are the keepers of the breach."
A belch: "I stay here until the next comes in."
Myself: "Then why is it I should hold my speech?"

We commenced walking as Regan endured a dry heave.
"You are the equal of everyone you see.
You must allow them to be what they are to be.

You must allow them to play their scene and leave.
Please hold your tongue and test what you believe
In the silence of your own conscience." My teacher

Did not look at me, but kept up a stern pace.
"I'm at your service, but I'm not delivering
The answers to your questions. Instead you must face

The very shadow of your quivering
And acknowledge the strength of its force and its weight
Even as you attempt to stem its shivering,

When there is nothing there for your body to hold."
I thought for a moment and said, "I don't get it."
"If you hold your peace, you may discern some gold

Among the fool's stones and the sickening vomit."
I knew better than to assert anything bold:
"Show me the way Uncle. I will be honest."

We came to a red door which bore an inscription:
"Forsaken." My guide: "Even if this is true,
You remain of the earthly anthropomorphification.

You are not one of the elected to be strewn
Into the hell of this bureaucratization.
Have no fear of the words which you are shown."

We entered a simple door and sat in an office,
The like of which one might see in a lobby.
But all about there flew a plague of locusts   (195)

Such clouds that I could hardly breathe or see.
Certificates hanging said 'Herbert Hoover Insurance –
Registration required and Be Seated.'

The line behind us extended for hours
And I perceived a mounting frustration
As if I had it within my powers

195 - ...all about there flew a plague of locusts...

To know the stress and knotting tension
Of those hungry masses crowding in the Bowery,
As if they knew that there was no cessation

(Of their stomachs as aching hollows)
To be found as they waited for assistance
Which would not be forthcoming tomorrow.

I felt deep ignobility and indignance,
The very face of which was creased and sallow,
Rumbling through the guts of a mob of resentments.

After as many hours as have four score
And seven years, a round but haggard man appeared.
We were all starving and ill but Lincoln forswore

To hassle further this mole in the veneer
Of a rotund man who could not see further
Than the dusty whiskers of his squinting sneer.

"I believe," extemporized my avuncular guide,
"That we are free to pass by this office." "Oh, no!"
The spongeular, homogenized president cried,

"None may pass without registration." "But though
We have been here the hours of years, you try
To exert your influence against the overthrow?"

His round face tilted over his round body,
And a bead of sweat dripped off his nose.
"I've got the guns and the numbers, so nobody

Gets through this office without one of those."
The light was so red and my head imploding
With the hunger of famine and wasted plows,

I did not see the paper before us, a legal
Document, indemnifying said agents
For services rendered, requiring signatures

Prior to embarkation. My guide read the contents,
Took a pen from his pocket and served imprimatur   (233)
For a further broadening of our horizons.

233 - My guide...served imprimatur.

Hoover's vacuum of eyes went out like they pulled a plug
And there was nothing. He mumbled some and grimaced.
He rubbed his bald head and jumped when the water jug

Bubbled up ominously. He looked like a man flummoxed,
Dammed up inside, condemned, and unable to shrug
The liquid weight of words which were heard promises.

I watched him and thought to call his attention
To the lines of thread-bare souls who were waiting,
Whose lives hung on their bones with the same attenuation

I: "There are more who come after us." My guide,
Who had undivided, with his will, a nation,
Interjected: "So we will be on our way, thank you."

Sweating he turned back into his office and more
People took our places and the line slithered.
As we passed wordlessly through the door

My leader cast glances at me which were withering
I remembered then what he had told me before,
I should be listening and not blithering.

And a vision blistered through my consciousness –
A dream as I perambulated –
Of this man being born a Kentuckian

And then to Missouri having emigrated,
Where masters and slaves were the lay of the land.
I did see a nation devastated.

And he had not spoken. Divided union I scanned,
Where brothers kill brothers with limbs amputated, (260)
War ceaseless between them, each of them damned

260 - Where brothers kill brothers...

To cursing revenge on the other, whose mother
And sister were raped by the brother, who will
Always avenge for the sins wrought upon him.

Complete I saw millions maimed and killed
Who might otherwise be of service as lovers
With soft hands, whose beards are anxiety ridden,

Whose kisses might be shared as generously
As the ballistics which rip the forests to shreds.
The man beside me was a savior as venerably

As the souls bayoneted, dying septic deaths
In the fields and the cities of the land of liberty,
But unique in manner and words and sense.

My silence was now his only prerequisite.
I could not even interject mindlessly
As was always my most exquisite

Pleasure, in polite intercourse with society.
When I was most empty, I was most expressive
And so I got on fine, until finally

People started catching me up in my lacking.
Lincoln would have to be one of those types.
But at thirty-five, one might begin relaxing,

And when in such company, who, without hype,
Proved himself at the level of the most exacting,
It was necessary for me to stuff my pipe.

Which was much less easy to do as we turned left
Down the hallway, found the door marked 'Dissolution,'
And we entered to discover behind the desk,

Shaded ethereal red in florescent diffusion,
Who shone so brightly from the deserts of the west
Across the screens of so many in need of illusion.

Three youths, as if they had never died, greeted us
With shine emanating through their welcoming smiles,
"We are pleased you are with us. You may be seated as

Your paperwork is processed through the archival files."
The woman spoke first, sadly, sultry, and baited us
With baleful sighs, "I hope you can stay with us for a while.

Things get interesting here in the evenings.
Somebody's always coming over with some wine.
We have a good time, even when we're working."

She giggled and one of the young men sang
With a southern twang, "I recognize this gentleman.
I'm sorry, but may I ask you to sign?"

He pushed a clipboard and pen over the counter.
"Yes," said the other, with more space in his voice,
As if he barely contained within him the power

To hold back the wide windy plains of his soul's choice,
"Mr. President. What brings you into our bower?"
"This young man is journeying to better know his joys."

"He's not so young," said the rebel in the red jacket.
The blonde woman cooed, "Nor does he know where to find joy."
The southerner frowned, "I ain't never seen nothing like it."

And I was made to remain silent and poised
As these icons pondered my fate. I was too attracted
To the woman, at whom I could not be annoyed.

Helpless as ever with these stars before my eyes,
I could not speak across the vastness, nor reach
Over with my sympathetic, pitying sighs.

She would never be mine, though I might beseech,
Though I might strain my throat with heavenward cries.
My guide surmised my wonder and turned to teach:

"Each and every night this trio of angels dies.
Recollecting all that they are leaving behind,
Fully aware they betrayed their promises.

They weep and they claw at their eyes, which are blind.
They intoxicate and metamorphize
Into fears which drive the clocks to unwind."

"I overdose on pills and alcohol."
"I drive my car into a telephone pole."
"I have a heart attack in the toilet stall."

"No one can love me but for my hole."
"No one can see that I'm an empty shell."
"No one can see I'm not king at all."

"So they die," said my friend, "With no one to save
Them. With nothing but what their emptiness gave them.
No intercession to deflect them from the grave.

Nothing but pity for what might have been when
They first gave themselves to the crowds of waves,
Before they became what they couldn't sustain."   (338)

338 - Before they became what they couldn't sustain.

"Here's your paperwork, Mr. Lincoln," Norma said.
I loved her more than I ever did before.
And the two other men, I loved them dead.

And I wanted to give myself to be their whore,
So they would know they could still buy a friend,
Or someone else they could too briefly adore.

As I reluctantly exited the room
And went down to the left to the next office over,
My guide noted the scarlet hue of my gloom,

Said, "Young man, anyone can be a lover.
Fewer can actually love themselves and exude
That love to the others with whom they endeavor

To make intimate contacts." I chose to remain silent.
He stopped then outside the door to look at me.
"You cannot fail, but you must be endurant.

You may speak, but you may find words unnecessary."
"Thank you," I said, for once feeling aspirant –
To see instead of being seen, impressed me.

My uncle pushed open this door and all vision
Melted and sweltered in a room of wet glass.
We had hardly stepped in when fire and adhesion

Drew us gasping into its maternal, molten grasp.
I straightened my back and panicked to breathe in,
Like a bug swallowed in a bubble of amber sap.

I felt the crystal heat flow into my throat and lungs –
Terror in my heart and eyes, Lincoln reached to touch me.
"What feels like lava, might very well be dung."

Which didn't make me feel any better, but trusting
In the prophetic quality of words from his tongue,
I could not fail, and so wanted to know his teaching,

That I ceased to resist not breathing and felt fine,
Like I had returned to a place previously known.
I wanted to reassure my friend and guide

But our movements in the magma were slow,
And my eyesight was glazed over, though not quite blind.
I spoke no words, waited to see what my guide would show.

There were no walls but the limit of my reach
And the pressure on my skin. I could not but submit.
What I saw challenged my belief.

Floating all around me, in aimless, careless drift,
Dozens of bubble fetuses in sculptured relief.
I wondered how these creatures could subsist.

I wondered what it could mean that they were here,
Ontogeny recapitulating phylogeny,
When I noticed more beginning to appear,

And found that they were gathering around me.
I say, on the whites of my eyes I felt the searing.
Still was compelled to their praying; my guide stood between.

One of the children stared: "We've not seen a breather."
My leader replied, his voice carrying through lava,
"Good children, we are not free to stay, but neither

Have we passed without signing off." "You are supposed to
Register every soul who enters. Did you see Hoover?"
"Yes, we spent a great while on that bother."

Then one child approached me very closely.   (394)
"Nobody here cares about signing off. We should
Be presenting the atmosphere falsely,

If we were to say there was not any good
In being kept out of heaven most grossly.
We ought to try to be better understood."

"You mean to say that you are, all of you, sinless?
That you…" I could not go on. "We are the souls
Who have accumulated from the beginning,

394 - Then one child approached me very closely.

Who never saw the light of day, but who know
A world of blood sensations, red illusions,
And who must be held away from help to grow.

There is no Elysium. As you can see, we are
Defenseless as gatekeepers." I know not how
I spoke: "Reagan said he was the gatekeeper.

And what of Hoover's endless room?" "There are now,"
The fetus communed gravely, "More of our weepers
Than there will ever be of that herd of cows.

I don't mean to be rude, but they have no grace.
They don't cherish a world of soft silence.
The Presidents come here and stir up the place,

Upon the dignity of their earthly offices insisting
That one of their own represent at the gates,
As if they could be more eloquent than children.

Satan was somehow persuaded, but then
They couldn't just choose one." "And what of Dissolution?"
"You can't withhold a flood, once the gates are open."

The child sighed and my guide bade me: "Our intrusion
Here is done." Without a name or word more spoken,
The child floated away from us. My confusion

Was profound. My guide opened a door and we passed
Back into the heavy spacious realm of air,
Where sound traveled with weight, I choked on gas.

Cold and on my knees on the carpeted floor,
"Is this the beginning of the journey?" I gasped,
As I vomited a phlegmy placenta there.   (429)

429 - I vomited a phlegmy placenta there.

For a pilgrim, there are many beginnings."
My knee jerked: "Hey! I am not a pilgrim.
I learned that from old friends, never submitting

Was the highest virtue we could build up."
"Do please spare me more of your reflectings.
All that must wait until beyond the end of it."

"Let me please ask what sense it makes to place
The souls of dead fetuses in a hellish mire?"
"There is no answer to that consideration."

"Who sent you to take me into this fire?!" (440)
I pointed angrily at him who smiled in my face.
"I am free to respond, but I fear you tire.

You let your emotions flare like hot dry grass,
With the sun baking down, in the summer
In a parched desert landscape waiting for rains.

You can't escape the spark which starts your burning up.
That is to say young man – I am here to sow the grains –
I cannot make them grow." "Thanks for summing up

Your duties so succinctly." A sense of shame
Overtook me as I let sarcasm boil
Itself into a quick and shadowy vaporous veil.

440 - Who sent you to take me into this fire?!

My uncle waved his hand and I saw no scene,
My eyesight was covered with a cloudy sheen
Which flickered in red in a hail of flame.

His tone was not ominous, but he spoke directly:
"Your intercessor is she whose love you most admire.
And if you asked, she said that she permitted me

To offer this display as the badge of her desire."
The hail of flame changed to rain and I felt relief   (458)
From the penetrating heat of the undying fire.

"Her request is that you give to your host the utmost
Of your faith." I: "I will." And the rain vaporized.
The furnace of the earth resumed its work to toast

The souls of those whose wills had froze to sample-size.
Ready to continue our helicular motion,
I still wondered for whom this hell was corporatized.

My guide was ahead of me turning left again
Down the hallway, he said: "Your Lilica will show
You how to fill in the spaces of your questions."

"In the meantime I am not able to know
Precisely what I am experiencing?"
"You know it even now, but you don't grow

458 - The hail of flame changed to rain and I felt relief...

Merely by knowing. The scenes change around you.
Other shadows have other stories. You must observe.
Nothing you see or hear should ever astound you."

I could not but consider the love of Lilica
As the *sine qua non* of this brazen adventure.
How could I proceed with other than humility?

I began to take pride in my noble indenture.
And the many who refuse to join with me
Will be left behind with little expenditure.

For there are indeed attractions in this progress
Down and to the left, particularly to non-believers.
Where my leader took me on in seeming digress,

Or sideways, spiraling, like a crab, or a spider, weaving
A dense fortress of silk, from which to commence ingesting
The separate abiding natures of all these perceivings.

Through another door, Uncle entered and turned to me.
Behind the door seemed an empty warehouse of silence;
Before I entered, he was facing me sternly.

I hesitated, yet, in randomness is exact science.
I stepped in to face what my leader spurned to see.
A light shined on me, I could sense the audience.

A warm bath flooded me, a fearful relaxation.
I cast a panicked concern toward my leader.
He seemed untroubled by the need for urination

Which I felt as someone who is always needier –
In golden swathes of liquid kisses and masturbation –
I wanted more, even as I had to tighten my bladder.

503-4 - ...whose shackles/Only appeared to be as fine as silken tassels...

Cheers erupted in the hall, cascading echoes
Of clapping hands and hailing calls and whistles,
Apparently for my having entered from the shadows,

And so I gathered in love, roses without thistles,
From a loving and respectful throng, whose shackles (503)
Only appeared to be as fine as silken tassels,

But would reveal themselves in momentary course,
As rather less than benign, yet not so much evil.
For the hall presently regained its mute force,

The crowd hushed in anticipation of betrayal.
I realized that they then expected performance,
The nature of which I was at a loss of retrieval.

"I don't understand," said I, and the crowd roared, (511)
A harrowing cry of mirth and ill-favor.
My spirit took flight again, on wings of praise I soared.

Glorying in the swelter, pungency, and savor
I felt for this humanity, which beyond its accord,
In union with my ego, also served as validator.

Their laughter and applause filled me with enough.
When they becalmed themselves again, they took on
The role of expectant lover awaiting the touch

Which I was less able to confidently discern.
I put my hands out gently and attempted speech:
"I don't understand." And the audience turned on

Their howling gush of comic climactic pleasure.
Awash again, these swells flooded my equilibrium.
"I don't understand." Cheers in crescendo,

511/22/25/31 - I don't understand!

"I don't understand!" Brought equal opprobrium,
And I wished before I had had the prescience
To know this would be more like the Colosseum

Than Carnegie Hall. They laughed and loved my sorrow,
The confusion on my ignorant and mournful pate.
"I don't understand!" Crashing derision, followed

By the scornful, merciless cries of the disappointed,
Fell upon me and I looked to my guide to borrow
Some knowledge to extrain me from the situation.

He gave me no words to soothe the stinging trauma
Yet his eyes said I was free to walk away.
So why would I want to stand and enact a drama,

For which I had not prepared a single day,
When I could be eschewing *la grande fama*
And getting myself ready for the next stage?

Not without a pang of self-pity did I leave,
For what greater virtue than fame in this age?
But Lilica waited for me, watching me misread

What must have been so clearly written on the page.
I was illiterate, misunderstood the cheers,
As if imprisoned without bars in a cage.

I opened the door myself and heard booing now.
My leader followed me and as I turned to wait
He tripped across the threshold, landing on a knee.

"Good thing 'twas not a sow," he said and commenced his gait.
Each step seemed now more downward, sinister, sideways.
The padded hallways were no less distortingly scarlet.

With my eyes as the center of focus, I felt pitched;
A fish-eye lens on top of a roller coaster
My nose and myself flailing, crashing in a ditch,

Upside down and gaggingly disoriented.
Yet I landed nowhere and remained in one piece.
Soon I felt the hand of the great emancipator

Lifting me only toward him and felt no need for balance.
I felt his lank body, the width between his ribs.
Sinewy fingers and arms held me to his phallus –

The power of the man, though of course he was flaccid.
(Sizing people up has always been one of my talents.)
In this case he was the active and I was the passive.

Who among you refuses love? Then you are corrupted.
I could not see straight and was made ill;
This man was carrying me and I interrupted:

570 - Young man, you will have your fill.

"How far is it to the furthest point which we will
Reach when we get there?" He kissed me and erupted
With laughter. "Young man, you will have your fill."   (570)

We entered through a door and gravitation
Rejoined us on the other side. I could see,
But my vision spun in gyroscopic wavelengths.

My head ached and the red lights had bled into me.
We were in a hotel bathroom with the sauna light on.
Cramped and boiling, I regained sensibility

To watch myself enter the room and sit on the john.
I remembered this scene, on the road, near El Paso,
Lilica was sleeping on the other side of the door.

I started to scratch at my scrotum, then turned on the fan.
Rifling through Lilica's toilet bag, I found her brush,
And spent fifteen minutes fiddling with that bow

Upon my instrument, which was more proudly erect
Than I was as I rubbed my skin the raw color of meat.   (584)
Eventually this ended and the muscular play

Began. Some slap, some tickle, a little more scratch…
When I got my rhythm and then ejaculated
Into my hand, both of my minds thought, "This is hell."

But as I watched myself wash my hands,
I thought why can't I enjoy such indiscretion?
Why must shame be my greatest demand?

Lilica had warded off my insinuations,
Am I not the lord and master of my domain?
As I turned off the fan, I felt compassion

For me, because there is neither right nor wrong.
"Son, do you believe you have seen love?"
My wits were not ordered, I could not move my tongue

Nothing more was said. We went on in a shrouded fog
He kept close, yet did not turn back to me once;
I pictured living in a cabin made of logs,

Which you hewed yourself, for your own benefit
(I am the meek inheriting an earth not so unlike
The different world of which I was then inhabitant,

584 - I rubbed my skin the raw color of meat.

Surreal dreams and the crippling deliverance of earthquakes,
To provoke the nostalgia of past ammunificence.)
A log cabin is the last place a man can be unquiet.

But he found discord and melancholy
In the clapboard houses of the state capitol.
He discovered his reaction to fools and folly,

Where society embraces the vapid, all
Of whom have bullets of opinion to volley,
Toward the leader whose fated and rapid fall

Is approaching him as he walks toward it
I had been weighing heavily on my guide.
I could do so easily, yet he could not ignore it –

The great responsibility of leading the blind
To the point where they can understand their world – it
Appeared to me momentarily, and then belied…   (618)

No longer in any hallway, my Uncle opened
Another door, strange for the ornateness of its carving,
And gave a mighty push with his left hand.

Vermilion brilliance generated behind a curtain.
We entered a ballroom full of old men
Doddering, wandering, dressed alike and uncertain

617-18 - it/Appeared to me momentarily, and then belied...

When the next heart attack would suddenly strike.
In thin plaid robes and padded slippers shuffling,
Muttering of the glories of the bloody pike,

They swung their nuclear arms as if they were putting,
With wrists held to crotch, inverted profane prayer, like
The membrane of the frog's throat, puffing and shutting.

Entitled to drive his balls down into the canyons
Or up into the space where heaven used to be;
Somehow unaware that his body has abandoned

The will to power of the spirit which used to see
Millions below him; like Lear in the conundrum
Of when his heedless daughters refused to be

The embodiment of his ideal. Yet these men were bald.
Several of them bumped into us incoherently
Mumbling about brinksmanship and Berlin walls

One who was more lucid approached us, apparently
He recognized my guide. "Mr. Lincoln," he called
As he smiled and put his hand out handsomely.

"Please," my Uncle pushed away his gesture,
Pointed to me: "I am this man's guide. Please
Tell him the story of your near departure."

Dissatisfied though he was, he turned and wheezed,
"I was a hero. I say it not as forfeiture
Of humility, merely as a staging for the scene –

I knew the drudgery and exaltation of conquest.
Laurels rested upon my head, I tasted greatness
As validated by the crowds who watch the contest.

652 - ...they loved me for my fatefulness...

My men, well they loved me for my fatefulness;   (652)
That is why they willingly perished in the bloodfest.
Because they had no means to escape their gratefulness,

If they but lived through the drama of my creation.
Certainly none can say we were less magnanimous
Than the cowards we drove into abject retreation.

Still, prior to that, my life was unglamorous,
Desks, telephones, meetings. Maps, numbers, preparations
Now my acclaim is virtually unanimous,

But for the enemy, who were always a poor ally.
It is better to see the enemy's bare face,
Than to join in alliance with a spy."

Not perplexed, but satisfied, I needed no more speech.
My guide stood also. Ike seemed to wish to say good bye;
He saluted and disappeared into the space

Occupied by the soft-footed mannequins,
One could not say they appeared to be tormented
But their motions possessed clamped and frantic spins

To which, with a hand to the chest, they all responded.
My guide: "Have you seen enough here, young man, of these sins?
Are you ready to move on?" I said, "He relented

More readily than I might have expected."
"Where nature leaves a lacking in its forms,
The manifestations are evident but neglected.

That is to say that those who have identified norms,
Are the ones who most often fit the constriction,
And authority is no measure of the truth:" My warm   (678)

678 - ...authority is no measure of the truth.

Uncle spoke and I tried to let the unknown be;
To not be afraid. To try not to know.
Because I did know, even though I could not see

(A sequence was repeated in hexagonal), (682)
Exactly the entire structure of the web we weaved.
What need I fear what was to come, if you

682 - A sequence was repeated in hexagonal.

Lilica, were the aim of my labyrinthine path,
And my guide was so true? Despite my insecurity,
I felt assured that I was not being asked

To understand. I was being made to feel irony,
And to not loathe its truth, to accept this faith,
That I not choose between ugliness and beauty.

Was it for me to feel like I was losing
Something precious? What purpose would tears serve?
I left the Eisenhower room musing

Over what fear had ever done, but shatter nerve.
And that nerve is much more grand than confusing
What might have been with what one deserves.

Silence had begun to empower me to believe
I could comprehend the breadth of my surroundings.
I looked forward, more confidently, to seeing

The next absurdity in which these halls were abounding.
And when we entered, down and left, we were besieged
By Harry Truman and three more who were astounded,

"Tell us why you are here, Mr. Lincoln," Truman inquired.
My guide shook no hands and offered no pleasantry:
"There is no reason I am here, but as this man's guide."

"Roosevelt didn't call for you?" one asked petulantly.
My Uncle flushed with anger, "He may have tried,
But he has not the power to harken me from purgatory

To this infernal honeycomb." Truman spoke fondly,
"Don't worry about Wendell, he's a Manichean.   (710)
Tell us though, is this young man still in his body?

710 - Don't worry about Wendell, he's a Manichean.

Who is he who comes into our tragedy, and
Who does have the power to force on you this bond?"
He: "I am sent by Lilica's beneficence.

It is she who has divine intentions for Fing.
As to who he is, that is his story." He turned
To me and bade me speak, but I had nothing

To confess because I hadn't yet learned
My story. I wanted to hear more from him
Who seemed to know the way and the purpose.

"How?" I began, but my Uncle touched my arm.
"Not now, young man, do you wish to use your time here,
To inquire of this gentlemen in their home?"

"Who are these three?" I asked of Truman. "I'm here
As one of FDR's vice presidents, whose harm
Was purely administrative, but I'm there

For other reasons." I could not decipher
His meaning. "You are banished for what exactly?"
"If you want some idea I think I can describe

By saying it was something we were lacking.
Not anything or everything. Nothing to die for.
Just something missing in the packaging.

And so we wait for a call to power
Which never comes. Although we are always ready,
The state functions without any of our

Assistance." "Do you resent being a figurehead?"
"I try to think of it as purgatory without
The motion. That way I'm less inclined to dread

The eternal aspect of this condition.
Things could be and are much worse for me, so
I try to enjoy the apprehension.

For the others, I suppose it is monotonous."
I: "I am at a loss of comprehension.
What did you do to be rewarded like this?"

"How can I know – or, by knowing, alter my fate?"
"But did you meet someone who brought you here?"
"I have always been here, and it's always been too late

To regret, so it's simple for me to have no fear."
"But isn't it a good thing not to be a slave
To wretched emotions which cannot endure

The plain scrutiny of reason?" "Reason?
No, I don't see reason winning in the end."
"And yet you just gave me a feasible

Explanation of the conquest of your emotion."
"Did I?" A door on the other side peeked open.
A voice spoken quickly, "You may see the President."

Truman and his accomplices jumped before us,
Throwing elbows and jostling each other.
When they fell to fisticuffs they ignored us

As we passed them by and went to see FDR
In the Oval Office. He was wheeling toward us
In his creaky wooden seat, with a blanket over

His atrophied lap. But he was barrel-chested
And broad-shouldered. He was chuckling aloud,
And grinning, looking up through his pince-nez,

"Abraham Lincoln, I presume." He put his hand out.
My guide took his hand and said, "It is a pleasure   (767)
To make your acquaintance." They were both proud.

767 - My guide took his hand and said, "It is a pleasure."

Then my emotions were shaken at the lifting
Of this veil. Again the world was not what it seemed;
I lost the balance of my equilibrium shifting,

And cross-eyed, collapsed across the carpet seams.
I wakened to the same two, newly met, assisting
Each other in attending to me and my dreams –

Where I saw Romans gripping each other's wrists
And laurels resting upon one cripple and one farmer. (775)
They formed a lattice held tight in their fists

775 - ...laurels resting upon one cripple and one farmer.

To use as foundation for an empire.
They were the fulcrum around which the helix twists,
Each bearing the comportment and sign of the palmer.

They gazed at the red skies and held the clouds at bay,
While I shook my head and breathed in salt vapors –
And I became aware again of nothing to say.

To behave as if I were muted by vespers,
Rather than to attempt to communicate;
I wished they would continue with their whispers.

FDR: "Now, young man, you've just got to suck it up!"
He inhaled deeply, "Come on, now!" He slapped my knee.
"Yes. Ok. Do either of you care that this is fucked up?"

"What?!" exhorted Lincoln. "Pacify yourself, Mister Fing."
"This has never happened before. I'm just all mucked up."
"What?!" said FDR. "Are you afraid to make history?

We need you, your pleasure, to complete our triangle
Of power and knowledge." My guide spoke plainly too:
"We can only communicate through your wide-angle.

It is my duty to be your guide. You search vainly through
Reason to bring you to the right angle.
I implore you to remain engaged to

The manner of our conversation. Just ask questions."
"Why are you in hell?" FDR: "Is that where we are?
I thought we were in Albany. Same sorts of vexations.

But seriously, one cannot always help – fear is fear
Itself. It's what the state uses for taxation –
Still I would never have guessed how far we were

From the welcoming embrace of paradise.
One does the best one can in one's own milieu.
Of course, there were some injustices and handicaps,

As I'm damned, there's no need to lie to you;
I only utilized the technologies
Available to me and the European retinue.

I ruled the greatest state known to mankind
In its most shining hour. What should I care
Where I'm relegated afterward? It would be fine

To exist in a cushiony place, where
No challenges propel one to follow a line
To wherever it ceases to go, to not dare,

But that was never my fate. And what of you, sir?"
We both looked to my guide, and he hesitated.
"This is half my journey, but he goes one third further."

FDR sat still, but his eyes calculated;
Then he nodded in a puzzled bewilder:
"Meaning, you are not unlike us deviated.

How can it be that *you* are held apart?"
Uncle furrowed his wide brow. They were both looking
At me while they spoke. I was at the heart -

Like the medium who presides at a sitting,
I was both empty and necessary, like the cart
The ox drags to market for resupplying –

Of their ability to transcend time.
"Time!" Our persevering elder interjected
"There is no way to get beyond it. I'm

Not against greatness, if it is intersected
With humility, of whatever source. But blind,
Headlong racing, such as we manifested....

Well, the reward is not eternal glory.
Lilica will be the love which means freedom.
New beginnings, the revolution of the story

To the final, and first, stage." I had to be dumb:
"Final *and* first?" FDR seemed to see: "Or we
Might refer to the phrase 'e pluribus unum.'

Implosion creates explosion. Paradise is action.
And all the rest is *ressentiment*, second-guessing."
I: "I think you gentlemen are ahead by a fraction

Of the capacity of my mind. What time is it?"
They laughed and looked fondly at one another.
Paternal and patriarchal, humbled by fine wisdom,

Each accepted their bittersweet discovery –
They spoke in unison, "Time to continue."
They bowed briefly to each other,

Clasped right hands and smiled, speaking no further words.
My guide turned and I stood to leave. "Thank you," I said
To FDR. He: "It's been nice for me too. I've never heard

Of such a thing. Feel free to come back Fing, again."
I was alone in the Oval Office with FDR.
I hugged him with a tear. He said: "Don't be afraid."

I left through the door my guide had left open
And I was back in the hallway with my guide,
Who was down and to the left, for the ground was broken.

He dried his face and did not attempt to hide
The tears he had shed for his condemned cousin.
I stood with my tongue swelling inside

My mouth, I could breathe, but my voice was cut short,
And no other sound emitted than the humming
Coming from the chords at the top of my throat

I felt in my muscle the throbbing of drumming
My own blood pulsing, like the flame of a torch,
Far away in the black night of wondering

About the manner of my response to this dream.
For, despite the boundless irrationality,
An unrelenting discipline is what it seemed;

A lesson to conjure into rationality
From that which was so inarguably deemed
To have been of import to my nationality

In the presentation of what I had seen –
Thus far...*E io a lui*: "Sir, I must admit (875)
To some weariness. I hardly remember where I've been

And cannot imagine what more could exist
In these scarlet halls. For the moment, I would be keen
On finding a door through which we might exit,

875 - e io a lui

And I could sit down and gather my wits."
My guide was in no mood to debate the matter:
"Stand up, young man, and remember Lilica awaits."

"Please sir, I mean no harm, but I would be gladder
If I could prepare and pace myself for the next affects.
Do you know how much further we will wander?"

He: "I am your guide. You are on a journey.
You are free to stop, but the journey does not.
And if you stop, you will take the path of injury,

Whereby you will not be lead to Lilica (who has not
Asked me to be your guide to *that* ignominy).
You must of your own free will cease this plot,

By the recitation of a single word."
He said no more. And I saw the bait hanging
There before me. My fish instinct said 'Take the worm.'

But then I thought about the hook which was hiding
Inside the meat of my guide's silence. It would be absurd
To anticipate the savor of that knowledge, knowing

The pain which must be delivered with the pleasure.
"I am ready Uncle. Lilica believes in me
I am wrong to think I'm at my own leisure.

I want to do my duty to those who conceived of me.
I hope you can forgive my cracking under pressure."
"Lilica awaits, " he touched my shoulder, relieving me

Of my most immediate fear, his disrespect.
Then he passed through the next door. I could no longer
Afford the indulgence of my misperceptions.

As if I were a cold and embittered fish-monger,
I had to accept the smell and the conditions,
And progress by digression through the bog water

Of this perditious invention. Into the room
Septic and rank, I stepped and began gagging.
Vomit burst from my guts in a vermilion spume

And splashed on the stainless steel flooring.
Then I felt empty but for dread. In that gloom,
Stretched naked on a stainless steel gurney,

Lay JFK, his head and neck openly wounded.
Lincoln did not go further and we watched a nurse
As she, with determination in her manner, attended

To her patient's body with her chart. He was hoarse,
But I heard him say, "They said I was nearly mended.
I can't feel a thing. I can't feel a thing. This is worse

Than liver problems, I assure you." Then my guide
Walked out of the red shadows cast to the corner
Into JFK's sight, in the middle, under the light.

"My God, that's Abe Lincoln! He's never been here before!"
The nurse was equally flummoxed, but plied her suit.
JFK: "They are trying to revive me. I'm sorry

I don't have a hand to offer." His mammalian
Brain was spattered like unpopping bubbles
On the cold steel slab. The nurse clipping his nails,

His hands remaining nonplussed for her troubles.
Uncle: "Sir, I was this way before your arrival.
Do you know the best way to where the torment doubles?"

"You think it gets worse than this? I'd like to see it.
I have an open mind though. I sense others…
Who is your companion? I don't have any feeling!"

He shouted at the nurse, who said: "If I had druthers
You'd feel this." And she bit into his finger
Hard, like crunching the sandy gristle of a mollusk.

She was gnawing viciously and JFK muttered:
"I wish she wouldn't do that. But how did you come
To be traveling here?" "I don't know," I sputtered.

My guide cleared his throat: "He is to know what has been done.
Therefore we journey through this land of clutter
And unchanging distress, to better know what's to come."

I to my guide: "You've been here before? When?"
His only response was, "I was alone."
He turned and spoke to JFK, ignoring me then:

"Sir is the way in known to you or unknown?"
"I thought I *was* in, but the nurses have an entrance
Which might have a staircase spiraling down

To the left." I: "Mr. President, you were my hero,
When I was ten." He: "Ten is a good age for a boy."
"I think the negatives about you add up to zero."

He: "If only you were an omnipotent hoi polloi,
You could be my deliverance from this feral
State." "I wish it were so, but I am a toy

In some child's imagination, no more real
Than you are." "Sadly, we are all too real, and I
Must return to my resuscitation. I can't feel!"

He groaned, and we went through the nurse's door,
Down these steps which propelled me forward, like
My center of gravity was deep below the floor

And the central pole, to which I clung with my life,
Was spinning like a top which has yet to right its core –
The axel points drawing bent circles. And I felt spite

Well up centrifugally, an envy
Of Lilica's difficult orchestration,
And my guide's effortless, seemingly empty,

Reaction to the twisted machinations
Of our descent down such a plenty
Of stairs and cramping menstruations.

Nausea remained when the spinning subsided.
But my Uncle strode forward without symptom,
Through a red door with a sign: "Clothing prohibited.

All bathers must shower." I: "I feel fairly stripped of   (976)
Everything else anyway… Will you be exhibited
In a like manner?" "No," he smiled, "This fiefdom

Needs only to be witnessed. But you may speak
To the President if he is available."
It was a lockerless locker room of maroon brick,

With showers at the far end, which were discernable
By the odd plumbing. Rather than pipes sticking
Out of the walls protruded the unimaginable –

Fleshy noses, two feet in length, hung above the bathers
They twitched and sneezed and blew out profusely
An undiminishing flow of gelatinous boogers,

976 - All bathers must shower.

Under which each of the penitents stood grossly
Mortified by the crisp salty flecks which smothered
Them and caked in their hair, like slug slime, mucousy

And adhesive. Many left the locker room barfing.
I gagged as we hurried through. I knew I would too.
And I did as soon as we reached the wading

Pool. On my knees beside the railing, I puked
For all the injustices of my fathers and their failings,
As did most of the bathers, who, if they did not spew

Their stomachs, commenced to blowing snot into the pool.
I looked then all around the pool, layers deep,
Stood bathers expectorating and vomiting a gruel

Not unlike chicken chimichanga and tequila.
Then I saw the surface of the pool, a firm custard
Of defecatory ejaculations, a cornucopia

Of human effluvia. And one other man appeared
Who wore a full-body, black cotton bathing suit,
And encrusted pince-nez. His the stern face, flat, flaccid,

Of a great academician, his walk a weary gait.
Still he gazed at my guide as he approached;
He seemed to want to bear himself as a saint.

I stood, but the others continued their work.
He offered his hand to my guide, who said: "No."
He was affronted: "I am not any soda jerk,

But Woodrow Wilson, son of my father, whom you may know."
"I know not, but let this not cause us to murk
Our purpose with possibilities. Will you please show

This young man your everlasting punishment."
"Who is he that comes to see my performance?"
I: "I am on hajj to some unholy banishment."

Wilson: "I only speak the ideal language of Christians…"
"I am a pilgrim seeking career enhancement."
"Yes, that I understand. One must do unsavory things…"

I: "What is it that you are going to do?"
"I am the swimmer of this pool of excretions."
He swallowed hard: "It's something you get used to.

I am proud to do it, for self-determination,
For peace." Still the crowd around the pool extruded
Their urine and lipids. "For democratization."

He stepped up and dived into the semi-solid liquid.
His crawl was flawless and when he came up for air
Only small globules of detritus tipped in   (1029)

1029-30 - Only small globules of detritus tipped in/To his mouth.

To his mouth. But that was more than I could bear
And I fell to the side of the pool again,
Retching acidic bile onto the pile there.

Wilson pulled himself strongly and kicked with grace
Through the putrid gravy. I turned to my Uncle:
"What can this mean in proper time and space?"

He smiled: "Patience." "I feel like a blind spelunker,
And the cave is getting smaller, more fierce, more base."
"Trust not your senses, trust your release from this canker.

Trust Lilica. Let all the rest wait." Wilson flipped
And made his way back to us, his pince-nez still
Secure despite the thickness of the resistance,

Still encrusted, although he had eyelids drilled
Shut, anyway. He swam nobly and with stamina
Despite the accumulating putridity which filled

My esophagus with a bilious inflaming.
I looked back to from where Wilson had come
And then another man in a full-body bathing suit

Entered. He was shorter and stockier, a bull dog.
I did not recognize him as he scurried to his seat.
I pulled at my guide's sleeve and asked: "Another cog

In the machine?" "I do not know him, let us harken."
My Uncle raised his hand and the robust man strode
Toward us intently. "Will the night cease to darken?

Is this crimson landscape about to see blue blood
Again? Are you not Abraham Lincoln, the barque in
Which union was saved from secession?" Our guide:

"I am Abraham Lincoln. I attest to nothing else.
My purpose, and the intent of Lilica of love,
Is to allow this man to better know himself,

To take him to the tightest center of this winding hole,
Whereby he may see a reflection of his ideals,
And the shadows they cast upon his withering soul."

He: "I must shake the hand of Abraham Lincoln."
"This could not be your abode! You are Winston Churchill!"
I recognized the reedy tone of this rhetorician.

"You are British!" He: "Did you know that my mother
Was an American? A vivacious woman…
One might say that she laid the entire

Foundation of my career. And an American."
My guide seemed disoriented by this odd note:
"It seems this place has changed since my journey in."

"I used to come here often also." My guide did not
Return a hand for shaking, and Churchill let his fall.
"But then I took up painting and tick, tock –

I found peace of mind." I: "And yet you are here."
"Purely circumstantial. Nature's asymmetry
Shows us that formlessness is not a fault, where

Cosmos is generated by chaos. Specifically,
That is what we endure in every endeavor. We're
Always trying to normalize mutancy.

And this is the cause of our unhappiness,
When we could be embracing mutant normalcy.
And what is the difference? I leave to your guess.

I must continue with my penitence.
If one knows chaos, one can generate cosmos.
And so I swim through these effluvients."

He took his place and dove in when Wilson touched
The wall. Wilson scraped himself as best he could,
But the pince-nez atop his nose remained caked in crust.

He walked toward us with a shiver: "I should
Not leave without saying one more word. I must
Warn you that these is no such category as good.

Pursue what you will, but call it not goodness,
Lest you presume too much, and end with self-overcoming
Based on pride, empty validations, and the lewdness

Of manipulated desires, ripe for exploitation.
Think of what the road to hell is imbued with,
And find some other intent to go exploring."

He turned and did not turn back. Churchill was replaced
By Taft, whose dive was less graceful, but who,
With the hefty girth of well-fed justice, displaced

Inordinate volumes of the gelatinous goo,
Which sloshed onto the floor and drove us out,
The way we came. We slammed the door after we went through,

And heard the concussion of the liquid about
To break that door down. We kept scurrying to
The left and down, into a compression chamber,

Where my bones instantly began breaking,
My trachea cracked and my tongue and eyes bulged.
I felt my sinuses collapse and the aching

Pierced like a pin in my medulla oblongata.
My neck snapped and my skull disintegrated,
As I was given the vision of a Bulgakov.

I was brought into the presence of the prince
Of redness. And I knew my guide was with me,
But I was only able to catch a glimpse

Of the palm of his hand. Whether he was crushing
Or carrying me, I cannot say, but Satan
Was nearer to me than my guide. He shouted: "Pimps!

Pimps! Pimps! Ah, *ya no significa nada*!
Get Roosevelt on the line!" "I'm right here!"
A voice bellowed in reply. And then Satan,

Roaring like a bonfire, "Not you Teddy! (1123)
Isn't it enough that you are here with me?
Why do you insist on taking control?!"

1123 - Not you Teddy!

My sight focused impossibly upon the brash
And bully man, whose guts were strewn across
Space. Drones were eating them as if they

Were noodles in a bowl, tripe soup, for your hangover.
I: "Why are you most deeply damned?"
"I started this; that's why. But then Satan takes over,

And deceives you with possession of land,
Working machinations we can't possibly cover;
And all hell breaks loose. It's hard to walk softly and

Carry a big stick. You can say you are doing it,
But by the time everybody knows, you are
Not walking softly anymore, and an undying

Tax comes with that big stick. Time is on the side
Of decay. It is only presumption lying
About a golden age, or manifest destiny,

Or global capitalism, when we defy
The structure of Nature and cramp men into
Boxes with engines, with wires, with tires,

With appliances, with electricity.
I can't say I'm sorry, but I don't know
Why Satan prefers Eleanor's cripple to me.

He wears his enfeeblement like a badge.
If I could only have that horse under my
Control, there would be wind here again."

He raised his hands, but they didn't go up.
He groaned and we left him splayed as he was,
Like an insect pinned for dissection.

I began to feel as if I were hanging
Upside down, by a mucousy thread,
Like a slug copulating with another

Slug, except I was swinging with a pendular
Motion, slowly, across a widening arc.
And then at the peak of the widest swing

I was held fast and Harry Truman appeared.
I don't know how I knew it was Truman,
Because he was an open putrefying corpse,

Obviously melted by some intense force,
Incinerated but alive, and therefore food
For cockroaches. He did not speak but moaned:

"Oooooo. Ohhhhhhh. OOOOOOOOOOO."
"Sir, you have two punishments?"
"Oh, yes," he hissed in searing winces, "I

Remember you. Now you see better. Well
I suppose there is some justice in it after all,
I pushed the button that cemented this hell.

Ooooooooooooooooooooooooooooooooo.
If only FDR had lived another year. But you've
Seen his comeuppance. I'd rather be the worst

Sufferer in hell than to be Satan's lackey."
"Mr. Truman," I interrupted, "what does the
S. in your name stand for?" He said, "The same

As your D. I only did it for the look of it, like
Faulkner." "Oh," I was flattered, "You know
My name?" "I know all the names. From here I see

All. But if you can't stand the heat, get out
Of the kitchen, is what I always say. Although,
I can't really do that anymore. Ohhhhhhhhh."

Then he threw up cockroaches. I could sense   (1183)
The radioactive mist emanating
From his shadow. It burned my swollen eyes.

I commenced swinging again and the force
Accumulated precipitously
And the arc never seemed to come around

1183 - Then he threw up cockroaches.

Again. I knew it was almost over
And I wondered if I would now be killed,
Figuring I would fit into any one

Of several of these nightmares. My weariness
Tried to convince me that death would be alright.
But then I came to a stop again. It was Nixon.

I was not astounded. "Where else would I be?"
He asked nonchalantly. Satan appeared then, formless,
And he began to flay Nixon with his fingernails

Pinched together, stripping the skin so that blood
Seeped out into the space as steam rises from
Boiling water. With his other hand, Satan shook

Salt into his wounds. A caustic sizzle ensued,
Which tormented the howling President. He cried:
"Cover it up! Cover it up!" His skin blistered   (1200)

And bubbled a tarry resin. Satan took a moment
To look at me. "Any questions?" "If Nixon
Gets this treatment, what of Stalin and Mao?"

Satan tisked at me: "Everybody gets theirs."
"And what happens when you run out of skin
To peel?" "That hasn't happened yet."

"Where is my guide?" "He is with you, although
You doubt it. That is where I come in; when you
Begin to believe otherwise." "And how do I

1200 - Cover it up!

Get home?" "You are not going home, but I
Am now going to drop you into the river
Of cleansing fire. You will go over the falls

But you will survive, and your guide will meet you there
In order to continue your journey." I felt
A string snap and was immediately

In free fall. I did not recall my previous
Life. I could not see, nor hear; I felt only
The rush through wide open space, and the heat

Pressing my fragmented body. I made no
Covenants with myself, no promises,
No renunciations. I was not scared.

I wanted to touch the hand of Lilica,
To be relieved by the knowledge of her
Presence. And I knew it would come.

I wanted to see my guide again, so that
I would know that each step was bringing me
Closer. And like a wanderer, I wanted

To see the land I once knew, from which I
Had been exiled in this pilgrimage,
To touch that earth and look up at those stars.

About the Fictitious Author

D. Selby Fing (b.1941, Philadelphia PA—d. 1976, Philadelphia PA) was raised by his grandparents, after his father was killed in Pearl Harbor (just after he was born) and his mother left to find work during the war and to continue her life. His grandmother raised him to be a priest, and when he failed that, he became an itinerant poet and teacher who struggled with mental illness for the whole of his life. He met his wife, Lilica Del Rio, while hitchhiking from New Mexico to LA. They had two sons. Fing wrote *The Profane Comedy*, of which *Perdition* is part one, in the last year of his life, and killed himself on July 4, 1976. His second son, Y.S. Fing, is the motivating force behind this publication.

About the Illustrator

Seth Goodkind grew up in the scorching heat of southern New Mexico, but escaped to the mossy damp of Seattle, WA, where he is a cartoonist, illustrator and tattoo artist. He contributes historical and political comic strips about cults and crime to various underground publications, imbues his skin art with esoteric magick, and watches an inordinate amount of low budget cinema. His artistic influences range from Mesoamerican codices to Hieronymus Bosch and Garbage Pail Kids.

www.ingramcontent.com/pod-product-compliance
Lightning Source LLC
Chambersburg PA
CBHW060837170426
43192CB00019BA/2812